The
Middle East

the lands and their peoples

Maureen Ali

Macdonald Educational

Consultant Peter Mansfield
Managing Editor Belinda Hollyer
Editor Beverley Birch
Design Jerry Watkiss
Picture Research Caroline Mitchell
Production Rosemary Bishop
Illustrations Paul Cooper
Hayward Art Group
Maps Matthews & Taylor Associates
(pages 44–45)

J 915·6

Endpaper: Early morning on the bank of
the Nile at Luxor.

Contents page: Traffic jams the streets
of Mecca as pilgrims pray inside the Great
Mosque.

Photographic sources Key to positions of
illustrations: (T) top, (C) centre, (B) bottom,
(L) left, (R) right.
Bassem Abdallah 15(B). All-Sport 41(T).
Camerapix/Mohammed Amin contents page,
13(T). Camera Press 19(T). Mary Evans
Picture Library 17(BR). Fotomas Index
17(T). Robert Harding Picture Library cover
(BL&TR), 9(B), 11(TL), 14(T&B), 15(T),
34–35. Hutchison Library cover (C&BR),
9(T), 27(T&B), 29(B), 30, 33(T&B), 35(B),
40(BR). Iraqi Cultural Centre 34. Mepha
21(T), 39(T). Hugh Oliff 36(B). Christine
Osborne cover (T), endpapers, 10(B),
11(TR), 13(B), 26(BL&BR), 31, 35(T),
36(L), 37(B&C), 38(B), 40–41. Popperfoto
23(TL). Embassy of the State of Qatar 37(T).
Rex Features 18–19, 19(B), 20(T), 21(B), 22,
23, 24–25, 24(T), 25(T&B), 29(C),
(T&B), 40(B). Ann Ronan 17(BL). Ronald
Sheridan 9(T). Tony Stone Picture Library
(T), 38–39. Vision International/Paulo
Koch 11(B), 39(B). Jerry Young 41(B). ZEFA
12–13, 20–21, 28(B).

A MACDONALD BOOK
© Macdonald & Co (Publishers) Ltd 1980,
1987

First published in Great Britain in 1980 by
Macdonald Educational Ltd

This revised edition published in 1987 by
Macdonald & Co (Publishers) Ltd
London & Sydney
A BPCC plc company

Printed in Great Britain by
Purnell Book Production Ltd
Member of the BPCC Group

Macdonald & Co (Publishers) Ltd
Greater London House
Hampstead Road
London NW1 7QX

British Library Cataloguing in Publication
Data

Ali. Maureen
    Middle East.——New ed.——(Countries).
    1. Near East——Social life and customs
    I. Title   II. Abdallah, Maureen
    Smallwood.
    Middle East   III. Series
    956′.04   DS57

ISBN 0-356-13161-0

Contents

The land

Between Asia and Africa

Fifteen countries make up the area we call the Middle East. They cover about 6.4 square kilometres extending across southwest Asia to northwest Africa. The Mediterranean Sea lies to the west and the Arabian Sea to the southeast. The Red Sea forms part of the coast of Egypt, Israel, Jordan, Saudi Arabia and North and South Yemen. Iran, to the northeast, borders on the Caspian Sea.

The countries range in size from the gigantic Saudi Arabia to the tiny island state of Bahrain. The United Arab Emirates is made up of seven small sheikhdoms; Abu Dhabi and Dubai are the most important. The only non-Arab states are Iran and Israel (formerly Palestine) though the latter has a large Arab population.

Climate

In the northern region the climate is Mediterranean with hot, dry summers and mild, wet winters. In the deserts temperatures soar well above 40°C, though in the winter months a pleasant 15°C is normal. At night the level can drop below freezing. The deserts are dry, but along the coasts the heat is made more unpleasant by high humidity.

More than 100 million people

The population of the Middle East is well over 100 million. Most of the people are Muslims – that is, they follow the Islamic religion. In many of the countries there are Christian and Jewish minorities. Israel is the exception, having been established in 1948 as a homeland for Jews from all over the world. The Palestinian Arabs who lived in the area before the Jewish state was set up are now a minority in Israel.

Population density varies from place to place. The fertile strip along Egypt's Nile valley is one of the most densely-populated areas on earth, but the rest of Egypt is sparsely inhabited. In the Arabian peninsula human activity is concentrated along the coasts. The fertile uplands also have a significant number of inhabitants, but the desert interior is largely unpopulated. Across the north, in Israel, Jordan, Lebanon, Syria, Iraq and parts of Iran there is relatively high population density.

Similar yet different

The people have a variety of lifestyles. The routine of the city-dwellers in Cairo or Baghdad contrasts sharply with that of the Arabian peninsula or the mountain people of Iran or Iraq. Society is patriarchal and, overall, very traditional. Religion still plays an important part in daily life.

The Middle East

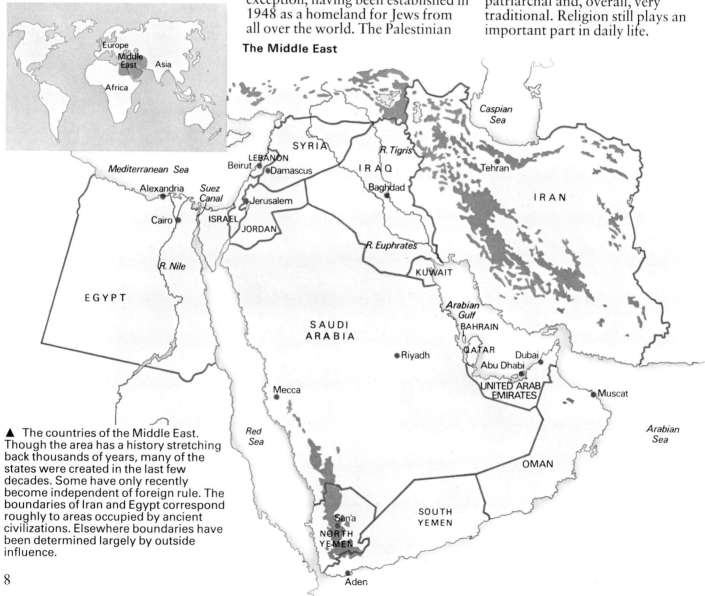

▲ The countries of the Middle East. Though the area has a history stretching back thousands of years, many of the states were created in the last few decades. Some have only recently become independent of foreign rule. The boundaries of Iran and Egypt correspond roughly to areas occupied by ancient civilizations. Elsewhere boundaries have been determined largely by outside influence.

▲ Barren desert covers much of Egypt and Jordan, southern Syria and Iraq, the Arabian peninsula and eastern Iran. This is the Negev desert in southern Israel. Though life here seems to offer few rewards, even today many nomadic bedouin people prefer the desert rather than moving to the city.

▼ The sea has always played a vital role in the life of people in the Middle East. The seafaring tradition goes back to the fifth century BC when the Phoenicians sailed from Lebanon and Syria to the west coast of Africa and beyond. The famous Sindebad launched his voyages from Oman at the southeast tip of the Arabian peninsula. In the Gulf fishing and pearl-diving were major industries before oil.

▲ The Euphrates river. The waters of the Tigris and Euphrates of Iraq and Syria, the Nile in Egypt, the Jordan and the Orontes and Litani in Lebanon, are all vital in an area where the climate is hot and dry. The rivers have always been the main source of water for crop irrigation. The earliest settlers made their homes near river banks and built irrigation systems and water-collecting devices. The role of the river is just as important today. The flow of water is controlled by modern dams which also generate hydro-electric power for industrial and domestic use. Elsewhere, ground-water supplies the wells which irrigate oases in the desert.

◄ In the highland areas of North Yemen or southwest Saudi Arabia terraces such as these allow crops to be grown on the steep mountainside. Elsewhere, such as in the plains of Syria and Iraq, there are large areas of irrigated and dry farming. Many areas of the Middle East receive less than 12.5 mm of rain a year. In the eastern Mediterranean areas and the mountains of Iran rain falls in the winter months. In the Yemen highlands most of the rain comes from monsoons which cross the Indian Ocean in summer.

9

People and language

The Arabs and their language

The original Arabs inhabited the Arabian uplands, in what is now Yemen. Later the term was applied to the nomads from the central and northern Arabian peninsula. As Islam developed and spread, so did the Arabic culture. Later the word Arab was used for all people of the Arabian peninsula, and beyond it, who spoke Arabic.

Among the Arabic-speaking majority, there are pronounced differences in dialect from one area to another and two forms of Arabic have evolved: the so-called classical Arabic, derived from the Koran, the Holy Book of Islam; and colloquial Arabic, which has its idiosyncrasies in each country. Speakers often fall back on the classical forms when addressing someone who comes from a different area.

Jewish population

Until the creation of Israel there were Jewish communities in most countries in the Middle East. As hostility between Israel and the Arab states increased, Jews were encouraged to emigrate to Israel and in some cases were intimidated into going. But it was not always the case, and small groups still live and work in the Arab countries.

When the state of Israel was established, huge numbers of Palestinian Arabs living there fled to the neighbouring states. Unable to return, many live in camps and ghettos in Egypt, Jordan, Syria and Lebanon.

In Israel the native Palestinian Arabs (Christian and Muslim) now form the minority. Hebrew has become the official language of the state. The rest of the population falls into two groups: Sephardic or oriental Jews who have lived in the area for hundreds of years; and the Ashkenazim, Jewish immigrants. The Sephardic or Arab Jews, as they are also known, were previously integrated into the Arab culture and to some extent they have retained a separate identity within the new state. The Ashkenazim come from all over the world. Some of them were refugees from European fascism of the 1930s, or survivors of the Nazi holocaust in which six million Jews were killed.

Ancient cultures

Like the Sephardic Jews, the Nubians and Copts of Egypt and the Assyrians in Iraq and Syria pre-date Islam. They have held on to aspects of their culture and heritage over the centuries.

In Lebanon and Syria and to some extent Egypt and Iraq, there are sizeable Armenian communities. Their members fled to these countries in the wake of the terrible Turkish massacres of the Armenians in 1894 and 1915. Though they were able to integrate into the host countries, the Armenians have retained their language, culture and religion – being one of the oldest Christian nations.

Iran and the Gulf

In Iran the largest single group of people are of Persian descent. Though they adopted Islam, they retained their language (which is called Farsi) and many aspects of their ancient civilization. Modern Iran also includes a number of minority groups. Among these are the Azerbaijanis, who speak a Turkic language, the Bakhtiars, the Qashqai and the Turkomans, all of whom are Turkic minorities, and the Kurds, who speak a language similar to Farsi. There are also Arabs, Armenians, Assyrians and Baluchis, who all speak their own languages.

The sudden developments brought about by oil wealth attracted immigrants to the Gulf countries from all over the Middle East and

▲ A Nubian boatman from the Aswan area of Upper Egypt. The Nubians are the descendants of a negroid people. They settled in the area and were then conquered by the ancient Egyptians around 3000 BC, but have retained their own culture over the centuries. When the Nile was dammed at Aswan the lake which was created (Lake Nasser) flooded much of the Nubian homeland. Villagers were moved to other areas, but for the ancient Nubian culture it was a great loss.

▲ A young woman from Yemen. Yemen's history dates back to pre-Islamic times when a thriving civilization prospered and the famous Queen of Sheba ruled. The people of the Yemeni highlands in the southwest of the Arabian peninsula are considered to be the original Arabs. They adopted Islam in the seventh century but have always retained aspects of their culture, including a unique style of building and colourful manner of dress.

beyond. Egyptians, Jordanians, Lebanese and Palestinians provided a skilled labour force for the growing economy. Some families have lived there for two generations, though they do not have the right to nationality.

Communities from the Indian subcontinent also settled in the Gulf, but even those born there may one day be required to leave.

▲ Kurdish women in national dress. The Kurds, a Muslim people of Indo-European origin, occupy the area where Turkey, Iraq, Iran and Syria meet. Their number is estimated at between 11 and 17 million. They have their own language and culture but no autonomy in the states where they live. They have tried to achieve national recognition. In 1945 the Kurdish National Republic was established in Mahabad in Iran. It lasted a year. In 1974, after a bitter struggle in Iraq, the Kurdish Autonomy Law was passed giving cultural and political rights to the Iraqi Kurds. The concessions meant little in reality. With aid and arms from Iran, some Iraqi Kurds continue to fight the Iraqi army. Some territorial gains have been made but success depends partly on the war between Iraq and Iran. Many Kurds within Iran are opposed to the regime there, but the Iraqi rebel Kurds have become dependent on Iranian support.

▲ A man from the Gulf coast of Arabia where many of the old traditions remain and are cherished. The people of the Arabian peninsula migrated towards the coast in search of pasture and water. Some settled and became fishermen or pearl divers and merchants; others continued their nomadic life in the desert areas. The older people especially still enjoy the desert pastimes of hunting and falconry. Fine falcons are still prized possessions.

◄ A Syrian student at Damascus University. Contrary to the popular image of Arabs as dark-skinned and dark-eyed people, there are a great many fair-haired, blue-eyed Arabs, especially in Syria, Lebanon and Palestine. Some are descended from the Crusaders who inter-married with the Arabs and stayed on in the area after their defeat in the twelfth century.

11

Religions

Birthplace of religion

The three great monotheistic religions (that is, those based on the belief in one god), Judaism, Christianity and Islam, were founded in the Middle East and the area holds special significance for worshippers all over the world.

Shrine of Judaism

For the Jews, Palestine represents the Promised Land pledged by God to Abraham 2000 years before Christ. The first great Temple was built in Jerusalem by Solomon nearly 3000 years ago, though it was later destroyed by invaders. The Western Wall of the second Temple, built before 500 BC, still stands and is the holiest shrine of Judaism. Though the Jews were later driven away from Palestine by the Romans and dispersed throughout the world, there has always been a Jewish community living and worshipping around Palestine and in the countries of the Middle East. The customs and traditions of Judaism reflect the early history of its peoples in the Middle East.

Early Christianity

From Palestine the Christian faith spread through the world. Christ was born in Bethlehem and crucified in Jerusalem. There his followers began their mission.

Many Christians in the Middle East today are directly descended from the early Christians. In their churches they practise ancient rites quite different from those of the Church of Rome. They include the Eastern Churches, which broke away from Rome in 1054 and retained autonomy under their own elected Patriarchs. There are also the Oriental Churches which rejected unity with Rome and also retained autonomy under their Patriarchs. Others, known as the Uniate Churches, are affiliated with Rome but retain oriental rites. There are also Roman Catholics, Anglicans and Protestants, who follow the usual rites of those churches.

Centre of Islam

Muhammad, the founder of Islam, was a trader in his middle-40s when, in 610, he experienced a revelation from Allah (God). At this time Christianity was about 600 years old and Judaism had been established for about 2000 years. The Arabs followed neither religion and were not committed to one god. Jews and Christians regarded them as infidels.

Muhammad was a contemplative man, concerned about the moral welfare of his people. He was on retreat in the mountains when the Angel Gabriel told him he was to be last in the line of prophets after Abraham, Moses and Jesus. God would give the final revelation to him. He was afraid, but as the visions continued, he began to preach.

The ruling authorities were disturbed by the new Islamic movement, for it rejected their pleasure-loving lifestyle. In 622 they forced Muhammad to leave Mecca. This departure became known as *Hijra* (migration). It marks the beginning of the Muslim calendar.

From its base in Mecca, Islam (which means surrender) became an organized religious force. Muhammad's authority and following increased, and his people finally conquered Mecca in 630.

Islam, a way of life

From sunrise to late at night Muslims began to observe a routine of prayer and devotion. Their faith is based on a system of beliefs and customs known broadly as the Five Pillars of Islam. These are: belief in Allah, prayer five times daily, fasting, pilgrimage and almsgiving.

The Koran is said to have been dictated directly to Muhammad from Allah by the Angel Gabriel. Together with the *hadiths* (words and sayings of the Prophet) it provides a guide for all aspects of life including marriage, divorce, justice and business. Muslims should read the Koran at least once. It is about the same length as the New Testament of the Bible. The legal system (*sharia*) in Muslim countries is based on the Koran. The details of law are interpreted by experts called *ulema*. Believers insist that any problem, legal or otherwise, can be resolved through the Koran. They seek to reassert the Koranic system.

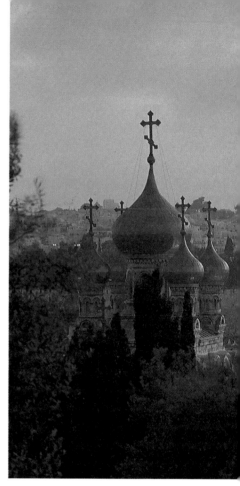

▲ Jerusalem, the holy city, is regarded as sacred by Judaism, Christianity and Islam. All have important shrines there. The Dome of the Rock is one of the most sacred Muslim shrines. It stands on Temple Mount, site of the ancient Jewish temple. The western wall of the Temple,

▶ The Royal Mosque at Isfahan, Iran, one of the great Shia mosques. When Muhammad died there was dispute over who should lead the Muslims. The next four leaders, known as caliphs, were chosen from the Prophet's family. When the fourth one, Ali, was appointed in 656 his rule was challenged by members of the Umayyads in Syria. He was assassinated in 661, the Umayyads seized power and the Muslims were divided. Those who followed Ali and his descendants became known as Shia (partisan) Muslims. The rest fell in line with the Umayyads and became known as Sunni (orthodox) Muslims. Today the Sunnis form the majority of Muslims generally, except in Iran, Iraq and Lebanon, where the Shias have the majority. Though the two branches of faith subscribe to the basic tenets of Islam, they sometimes differ widely in their interpretation of the Koran and in some religious ceremonies. Later other sects formed, including the Druse, Alawites, Ismailis and Zaidis, all of whom practise forms of Shiism.

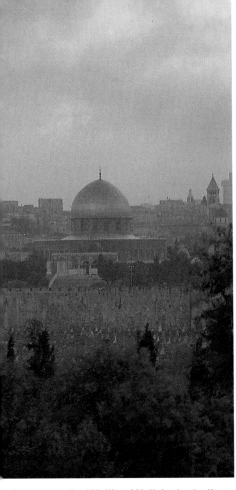

known as the Wailing Wall, is the holiest place of the Jewish religion. The Church of the Holy Sepulchre, where Christ was buried, is shared by six different churches, all separate from the Church of Rome. Pilgrims visit Jerusalem from all over the world.

▲ The Kaaba, in the courtyard of the Great Mosque at Mecca. Mecca is the holiest place of Islam, where the Prophet Muhammad lived and spread the word of Allah. Every Muslim who can manage it must make a pilgrimage to Mecca at least once. This pilgrimage is known as the *Hajj*. It takes place in the twelfth lunar month of the Muslim year. It involves very special rites including the temporary renunciation of all earthly possessions, fasting, prayers and devotions. Every pilgrim entering the holy city of Mecca has to leave behind all possessions and wear only two simple white sheets. One of the most important parts of the *Hajj* is to touch the sacred black stone contained in the Kaaba. In the courtyard of the Great Mosque thousands of pilgrims circle around the Kaaba for hours on end, making their way towards it.

13

Ancient civilizations

Cradle of civilization

In Mesopotamia, in what is now southern Iraq, some of the earliest remains of houses have been found dating back to around 7000 BC. In this same area the development of Sumerian culture, one of the earliest civilizations of which we have comprehensive knowledge, was under way around 5000 BC. When the Sumerians reached the area, the potter's wheel was in use there and a religion which included the worship of symbolic gods had been established.

The Sumerians built the city of Ur on a stategic site near the mouth of the Euphrates river. It developed into a thriving trade centre between the Indian Ocean and the Mediterranean Sea.

Waves of invasion

The Sumerians were replaced by a succession of invaders. Among these were the Akkadians, the Elamites, and the Amorites, who founded the kingdom of Babylon. The Amorite King, Hammurabi (1792–1750 BC) has the distinction of being the first ruler to devise and record a system of rules and laws. He regulated things such as land and cattle sales, water rights, canal maintenance and business conduct.

To the northwest of Mesopotamia (the area which now forms part of Syria, Lebanon and Israel) were the people known in the Bible as the Canaanites. They were followed by the Phoenicians. It was there that the basis of the alphabet was developed.

By 1466 BC an Indo-European people called the Hittites had occupied Syria and Iraq and were extending their rule over the rest of the area. The Hittite empire endured until around 1200 BC when it was replaced by the Assyrians, who remained in power for almost 600 years. They were the first outsiders to invade Egypt, reaching the city of Memphis.

In 621 BC the Assyrians were ousted by the Neo-Babylonians.

▲ Roman remains at Jerash, just north of the present-day Jordanian capital of Amman. Wherever they spread their empire the Romans built magnificent towns, temples and palaces as a testimony to their strength, wealth and power. Jerash was a flourishing Roman town which reached its peak in the third century AD. It boasted two amphitheatres, a beautiful temple dedicated to the goddess Artemis, and a triumphal arch dedicated to the emperor Hadrian.

◄ The marshes of southern Iraq are today the home of the people known as the Marsh Arabs. Man settled and built in the area 9000 years ago. Until recently, life for the Marsh Arabs had changed little since ancient times. Their reed houses, built on mud platforms in the marshes, were executed from a centuries-old design. They lived from the marshes, hunting, fishing, and tending water buffalo which they 'tethered' in the water. Sadly, the marshes became an area of conflict in the Gulf War and much there has been destroyed.

They were tough fighters who proved to be clever businessmen and skilled craftsmen. They set up a banking system and an export business in dates, wheat and wool. When the Egyptians tried to interfere in Syria and Palestine, the Neo-Babylonians invaded Jerusalem on two occasions.

By 539 BC the might of the Persians of the Achaemenid empire to the north was growing. By 530 BC they had conquered Babylon and Syria, and that year they went on to conquer Egypt.

Foreign rulers

The Achaemenid empire came to an end in 331 BC when the armies of Darius III were defeated by the Macedonians from Greece, led by Alexander the Great, who established control over the whole of the Middle East. From then on the area remained under foreign rule for centuries.

After the death of Alexander in 323 BC, the Macedonian empire was divided several times and ruled by various Greek dynasties until the Romans arrived in 188 BC. They waged a bitter battle for the area, but never gained control of Persia and Babylon. They were continually troubled by local unrest and in the fourth century AD rule from Rome eventually gave way to rule from the Christian Byzantine capital, Constantinople. Later this was superseded by Islamic rule.

▼ Remains of the city of Persepolis in the mountains of southwestern Iran. Persepolis was founded in 521 BC. It was developed by the Achaemenid rulers, Darius and Xerxes, as one of the capitals of their empire. Much of Persepolis was destroyed when the empire was overrun by the Macedonian armies of Alexander the Great, yet even today its magnificence is obvious. The relief work which decorates the walls is of high quality. It contains a wealth of information about the state of the empire, its history and importance. In its time the Achaemenid or Persian empire was the largest in the Middle East. Under the leadership of Cyrus the Great it spread out from Iran to Babylon and Syria. Under Cyrus's son, Cambyses,

Egypt was conquered. Under the command of Xerxes the Persian army seized Athens, which it held for a short time. The Achaemenid rulers allowed each kingdom to keep its own institutions, language and customs. The empire was divided into regions or *satrapies*. Each had a governor, a general and a secretary of state chosen by the emperor. Power was divided between them, and all three reported directly to the emperor. The provinces were taxed according to their resources and there was a highly-developed system of book-keeping. Inspectors travelled the empire on roads built primarily for their use. There was a well-disciplined garrison in every area so that if there was revolt it was quickly crushed.

◄ The people of ancient Egypt built huge monuments to their rulers. These are the Colossi of Memnon, which stand in the desert near Luxor. While various groups were fighting for supremacy in the areas of Iraq, Syria and Palestine, Egypt enjoyed a period of stability and prosperity. Around 3000 BC King Menes of Upper Egypt united his kingdom with Lower Egypt. The kings, or pharoahs, ruled Egypt for over 2000 years. Under them there was an efficient system of administration and taxation run by a central government. The kingdom was supported by a sophisticated agricultural system and defended by a strong army. There was a substantial knowledge of medicine. The arts developed, together with a unique architectural style. Among the surviving monuments of ancient Egypt are the pyramids near Cairo, the magnificent temples of Upper Egypt and the obelisks which now stand in Paris and London.

The spread of Islam

Conquest and conflict

Within 30 years of Muhammad's death (AD 632), the Middle East was united under the banner of Islam. From 661 the vast empire was ruled from Damascus by the Umayyads. In 750 the Umayyads were overthrown by the Abbasids. In 762 the Abbasids moved their capital from Damascus to Baghdad.

Though the Abbasids reigned as Caliphs until 1258, their power as rulers began to be undermined as early as 945 when the Buwayhids, a dynasty from western Persia, seized control of Baghdad. By 1055 the Seljuk Turks had taken over there. They defeated the Byzantine army in 1071, occupied much of Syria and Anatolia (central Turkey) and spread their empire eastwards to Persia. With the sacking of Baghdad in 1258 by Mongol invaders from central Asia, Abbasid rule officially ended.

Meanwhile in Egypt the Ismailis, later known as the Fatimids, had gained power. They founded the city of Cairo in 969 and developed it into an intellectual and spiritual centre to rival Baghdad.

The Crusades

When the Crusades to recapture the Holy Land for Christianity were launched from Europe in 1096, the Islamic forces of the Middle East were greatly divided by intense rivalry between the Seljuks and the Fatimids. In 1099 Jerusalem was captured, with the slaying of vast numbers of Muslims, Jews and even Oriental Christians. The Crusaders remained in occupation until 1187 when they were defeated by Salah al Din who restored Jerusalem to Muslim rule.

Invasion from the West

In Egypt Turkish influence was first established when the Mamelukes, a powerful group of mercenaries (who had originally come from Turkey as slaves), seized power in 1260. They ruled until the Ottomans from Turkey swept through the region and captured Cairo in 1516. Though

sometimes challenged from within the empire, Ottoman rule continued in many parts of the Middle East until the First World War.

The first serious threat to the Ottomans came with Napoleon's invasion of Egypt in 1798, as a first step towards gaining control of Britain's main trade routes to India. The invasion was a failure and the French evacuated in 1800, but the event was very significant. The British were alerted to the strategic importance of Egypt, and the Egyptians, who had been greatly impressed by French revolutionary ideas, were now less tolerant of oppressive Turkish rule.

Muhammad Ali

The Ottomans were seriously alarmed by the challenges which had been posed. They despatched a force to Egypt under an Albanian commander, Muhammad Ali. Rather than repress the Egyptians, Muhammad Ali gained their confidence and became the country's effective ruler in 1811. His growing power caused concern to the British, whose ambitions in Egypt were getting stronger.

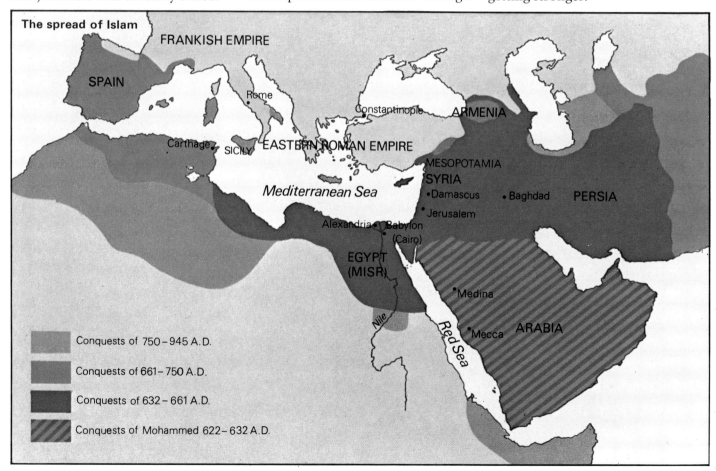

The spread of Islam

- Conquests of 750–945 A.D.
- Conquests of 661–750 A.D.
- Conquests of 632–661 A.D.
- Conquests of Mohammed 622–632 A.D.

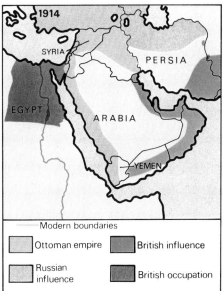

▲ A sixteenth-century Ottoman illustration of the campaign westwards. The Ottomans from western Turkey were descended from the Seljuks. They defeated the Byzantines in 1453 and spread their empire northwestwards into Europe, and south and east to North Africa and most of the Arab Middle East. Only the interior of the Arabian peninsula remained independent.

▼ A twelfth-century illustration of an Islamic chemist at work. Under the patronage of Caliph Haroun al Rachid (786–809), Islam entered its 'Golden Age' when the arts and sciences flourished. Baghdad became a centre of learning frequented by scholars from the Islamic empire. New scientific findings were recorded and works of literature, including *The Tales of 1001 Nights* were produced. Many of these were translated and widely used in the West.

◄ The influence of Islam spread quickly. Arabia itself came under Muslim rule before the Prophet died. By 750 most of North Africa had been overcome, and from there Spain was conquered. Muslim invaders reached Poitiers in France, before they were routed in 732.

▲ Before the outbreak of the First World War in 1914 the Ottoman empire ruled much of the Middle East. Britain and France had been rivals in the area since Napoleon invaded Egypt in 1798. Britain had consolidated her influence in Egypt, the southern coast of Arabia and the Gulf. Russian influence extended into northern Iran. Only the central Arabian peninsula and southwest Iran were truly independent.

▼ Muhammad Ali (1769–1849) challenged Ottoman supremacy in Egypt and became the effective ruler there in 1811. He made far-reaching changes in Egyptian education, industry and defence. When his authority spread into Arabia, Syria and Sudan the British moved against him in 1841 by signing a treaty with Austria, Russia and Prussia to curtail his ambitions.

17

Twentieth-century politics

The seeds of nationalism

Following the changes initiated by Muhammad Ali in Egypt, a new sense of nationalism began to develop. This first became apparent when the Egyptian army, led by Colonel Arabi, began subscribing to the slogan 'Egypt for the Egyptians'. Arabi's movement gathered such force that the British felt their interests were threatened. They invaded Egypt in 1882 and remained there for the next 70 years, with profound repercussions for the area.

Dissatisfaction with the Ottoman policies spread within the empire. When the First World War broke out in 1914 and the Western powers aligned against Germany and Turkey, the Arabs sided with the West against the Turks in return for promises of support for their nationalist cause. But at the end of the war in 1918, Turkish troops were replaced by the British and French armies, and independence for the Arabs was still far away.

Struggle for independence

The Arabs were often disappointed by their former allies and it was not until well after the end of the Second World War that foreign rule was eliminated from most of the Middle East. Even then, French and British influence remained strong and that of the United States began to become apparent.

The Arab struggle to come to grips with independence and to shake off the legacy of colonial occupation has been difficult and dangerous. Attempts to establish stability were often subverted both from within and by external interference from Western countries trying to retain their hold over the area or the Soviet Union trying to gain a foothold. The actions of President Gamal Abdul Nasser of Egypt against the West were inspirational in helping leaders in the Middle East to become aware of their potential.

Triumph and disillusion

In the early 1970s the Arab nations seemed suddenly to come of age. The notable performance of Arab troops in the 1973 war against Israel did much to boost morale in the area. At the same time, the Arab states realized that the oil they supplied to the rest of the world could be used to exert political influence. For a short time in 1973 they cut off oil to states which they believed were helping Israel. Oil production was curtailed and prices were increased to a level comparable with other commodities on the world market. In this way the oil-producing countries were able to convince the West that the days of exploitation were over. They were now determined to develop their potential as individual nations and as a regional power.

For a time an awareness of regional identity flourished and summit meetings were organized to try and define and consolidate the aims and policies for the area as a whole. But cooperation was short-lived. The Middle East was still beset with problems. Within a generation, some countries had passed from extreme poverty into a position of enormous wealth brought about by oil. There had been no time to adjust. The governments, representing every political ideology from absolute monarchy, through socialism, to Soviet-inspired communism, found it hard to collaborate with each other. There were extremes of wealth and poverty, and a multitude of cultural minorities striving for recognition.

Tensions grew and a series of events sent shock waves through the region. The outbreak of civil war in Lebanon had repercussions everywhere. Egypt recognized Israel and caused a major rift between the Arab states. The advent of an Islamic revival in Iran caused deep disquiet. The war in the Gulf beween Iraq and Iran placed great strain on all the neighbouring countries. The unresolved problem of Palestine continued to generate violence.

The political problems were compounded by fluctuations in oil prices and a drop in production. Economic recession set in. Industrial development in the Gulf was curtailed. Some businesses closed. Many government projects were shelved. Salaries were reduced and the work-force cut, with serious consequences for expatriate Arab workers.

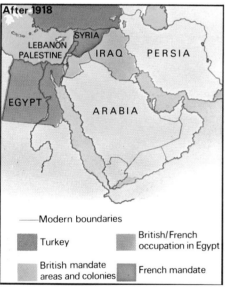

Modern boundaries

- Turkey
- British mandate areas and colonies
- British/French occupation in Egypt
- French mandate

▲ In 1916 the British and French governments signed the document known as the Sykes-Picot agreement. This arranged for vast areas of Arab land to be divided into spheres of influence under British and French control. It ran directly contrary to promises which were made by Britain to Hussein, the Sherif of Mecca, in return for Arab support against the Turks. The Allies' agreement formed the basis of the way territory was divided at the end of the First World War in 1918. Britain kept control of Egypt and Aden. Iraq and Palestine also came under British influence. The French took Lebanon and Syria. The region was to pay heavily for these foreign ambitions.

▼ Gamal Abdul Nasser of Egypt symbolized the spirit of Arab nationalism. He came to power in 1952 after a coup by army officers ended the corrupt rule of King Farouk. In 1956 he led the campaign in which Egypt took control of the Suez Canal from Britain. Though Britain, France and Israel attacked Egypt in retaliation, Nasser stood firm and called on Arabs to unite against Western colonialism. Intercession by the US and the UN forced the invasion forces to withdraw. Under Nasser Egypt began a programme of modernization and social reform. Though he is seen here (right) with the Soviet leader, Nikita Kruschev, Nasser tried to keep Egypt non-aligned, dominated by neither the United States nor the Soviet Union. His death in 1970 was widely mourned among all the Arabs. No Arab leader of equal stature has emerged to replace him.

▲ An Opec Council meeting. Because of their vast oil resources the Arab states assumed a prominent role in policy decisions of the powerful Organization of Petroleum Exporting Countries (OPEC). They used this influence to achieve political and economic gains.

▼ The civil war in Lebanon has developed into a battleground between all the opposing political factions in the region. The Palestinians, Syria and Israel have been directly involved in the fighting there, while countries like Iran and Libya have lent their support to various militia. Other Arab states have supplied finance to different factions. Western powers and the Soviet Union participated under various guises.

19

Palestine and Israel

Moves to establish a Jewish state

As anti-semitism against Jews increased in Europe at the turn of this century, the Zionist movement, which promoted the idea of a Jewish state, focused its attention on Palestine. A steady trickle of immigration by Jews from Europe was already under way there. By 1914 the Jewish community in Palestine had reached around 80 000. The Arabs numbered 600 000.

In 1918 Palestine passed from Ottoman rule to British control, and Jewish immigration increased. This was partly in response to the 1917 Balfour Declaration which promised British support for the Zionist cause. It stated: 'Her Majesty's government views with favour the establishment in Palestine of a national home for the Jewish people, and will use their best endeavours to facilitate the achievement of this object.'

The Arabs in Palestine had co-existed peacefully with their Jewish neighbours for centuries and had not objected to the slow immigration that had been taking place up till then. But they were naturally upset by the attempts of a foreign power to set up a state on their land, from which they would be excluded.

Conflict erupts

The pace of Jewish immigration increased over the next 20 years, at first with support from Britain. Arab resentment began to build up. In 1936 they took up arms against the British and the Zionists. Bitter fighting ensued in Palestine and, under pressure from the Arabs, Britain made some attempt to control the influx of Jews. Conflict continued until the outbreak of the Second World War, when an uneasy peace prevailed.

Birth of Israel

At the end of the war in 1945, and in the wake of the Nazi holocaust, illegal Jewish immigration to Palestine increased and violence resumed. Britain sought the help of the newly-formed United Nations. In 1947 the UN proposed an end to British rule. The UN plan called for two states to be set up in Palestine: a Jewish one on 56 per cent of the land, and an Arab one on the remaining 44 per cent. Jerusalem and the holy places were to be placed under UN administration. The proposal was rejected by the Arabs. At this time the Arabs numbered around 1.3 million and the Jews 650 000, with title to less than eight per cent of the land.

In May 1948 Israel declared itself to be an independent state. War broke out with the neighbouring Arab states. The fighting lasted until early 1949, by which time Israel held a greatly-increased area which included half of Jerusalem.

The state of Israel became firmly established despite continued opposition on behalf of the Palestinians. In this it has been helped by considerable support from the United States and by supporters from around the world.

Palestinian opposition to Israel was formalized with the establishment in 1964 of the Palestine Liberation Organization (PLO). This is the main voice of the Palestinians and it is recognized by the United Nations. Israel, however, condemns it as a terrorist organization, and refuses to have any dealings with it. The effectiveness of the movement has been impeded by internal conflict. The Palestinian National Council debates policy issues.

▲ Palestinian forces leaving Lebanon. In 1982 Israel invaded Lebanon in an attempt to destroy the power of the PLO which had grown to a level intolerable to Israel and some Lebanese factions. The Israelis advanced to Beirut where the PLO, supported by Lebanese allies, put up strong resistance. The world watched in horror as West Beirut was held to seige and subjected to frequent Israeli bombardment. A ceasefire was achieved through international intervention. PLO and Israeli forces were withdrawn from Lebanon. However the Israeli presence continued in the south and the PLO reinfiltrated. The war divided Israeli opinion unlike anything had ever done before. It weakened but by no means destroyed the PLO.

▼ In 1956 Israel invaded Egypt with support from Britain and France. Territories were seized but had to be handed back. During the 1967 war Israel advanced across Sinai to the Suez Canal, occupied the Golan Heights in Syria and the West Bank area of Jordan including Arab Jerusalem. In the 1973 war the Arabs made gains, but Israel later recovered most of the lost ground. In the Camp David Accord of 1978 the Sinai was returned to Egypt but Israel kept the Gaza Strip. In spite of this, the Arabs are convinced that Israel is bent on further expansion.

▼ The *moshavim* or agricultural settlements represent a success story for Israel and disaster for the Palestinians. They are built by the government to house Jewish immigrants on land often confiscated or compulsorily purchased from the Arabs. The settlement programme is part of a plan to develop occupied Arab land, especially in the West Bank area where 50 per cent of land has been taken over by the state of Israel. The water used on the highly-mechanized settlements is frequently drawn at the expense of the Arab peasant farmers, who are given only limited rights to sink wells or expand irrigation systems because water is so scarce. Their output suffers as a result. Many have difficulty sustaining their farms.

▲ A Palestinian refugee camp in Jordan. Many Arabs fled the fighting which broke out in 1948 and took refuge in neighbouring countries. When the fighting stopped Israel prevented them from returning. Nearly 40 years later many people still live in camps like this. They are stateless. They live mainly by casual work and on food rations provided by the UN. Many refugees were farmers and they still wait for the day when they will return to their land. There are about 2.5 million Palestinians in exile, some of whom have become rich and successful. Nearly another two million live under Israeli rule, in Israel and in the occupied West Bank.

▲ The signing of the 1978 Camp David Accord between Prime Minister Begin of Israel (right), President Sadat of Egypt (left) and President Carter of the US. In Autumn 1977 Sadat astonished the world with a visit to Israel to discuss the Arab-Israeli conflict. This led to the negotiation of the Camp David Accord which put an end to hostilities between Israel and Egypt. Israel handed back territory captured during previous wars.

Ambassadors were exchanged and trade was established. Sadat was accused of treachery by the Arabs and Egypt was isolated by an Arab boycott. Later Sadat was assassinated in October 1981 and Egypt's position was undermined when Israel invaded Lebanon. Relations between the two countries never fully recovered. There have been no other peace agreements. However there is now talk of an international peace conference.

Challenges from Iran

Independent culture
Since the time of the Achaemenid dynasty (558 BC) Iran has had a distinct culture with its own language, rituals and traditions. These were maintained after it was converted to Islam. Iran was never ruled directly by any colonial power, though it came under Russian domination for a while at the turn of this century.

Pahlavi dynasty
When Reza Khan seized power in Iran in 1925 and proclaimed himself Shah the following year, his mission was to rid Iran of foreign interference and restore it to its former glory. He built up an army which he used to suppress opposition, and began a programme of industrialization.

The Shah's ambitions did not take into account those of his neighbour, the Soviet Union. In 1941 a joint Anglo-Russian force invaded Iran and Reza Khan was forced into exile. He was succeeded by his 21-year-old son, Shah Muhammad Reza.

Shah versus the people
Like his father, the Shah felt he knew what was best for his country and would not tolerate opposition. In the early 1960s he embarked on a series of reforms referred to as the 'White Revolution'. Many of these, especially the sweeping land reforms, provoked protest. The army was used to suppress opposition and many people were killed. From this time until the Shah was forced into exile in 1979, brutal repression continued.

Iran had been among the first countries to force up the price of oil and increase its revenues. The Shah channelled these into industry and the armed forces in the belief that he could turn Iran into a powerful industrial nation. For the majority of Iran's 35 million people there were few practical benefits. The gap between rich and poor grew. The Shah became increasingly isolated from his people.

Revolution
Despite violent measures by the notorious SAVAK (secret police), opposition to the Shah increased. The clergy played a major role. They deeply resented the way the Shah's reforms undermined Iran's religious and social traditions.

With the powerful army at his command, it was thought that the Shah was bound to survive. But the opposition gained ground and people took to the streets in defiance. The Shah's allies in the West tacitly withdrew support. On 15 January 1979 he fled Iran.

Islamic republic
In February 1979 the Ayatollah Khomeini, who had led the opposition from exile in Paris, returned to Iran in triumph. Within weeks it became clear that the Ayatollah's demands for an Islamic republic in Iran could become a reality. The Islamic constitution based on the Koran came into effect at the beginning of 1980.

Opposition to the new republic was fiercely suppressed. Hundreds of people were tried and executed. Schools and universities were closed until new curricula had been devised. Thereafter they would be strictly segregated. Women were ordered into the *chador* (veil) and out of the work-force. Iran suffered but survived economic upheaval as it implemented a trade boycott against the West.

There were also many political casualties as different groups tried to establish themselves. A notable victim was Abol Hassan Bani-Sadr, first president of the republic, who fled to exile in France. Opposition groups exploded bombs in Tehran, one of which killed several members of parliament.

The outbreak of war with Iraq helped to unite the nation as it struggled to adjust to change. It also bought time for the government which was not ready to confront Iran's pressing social problems. Because of the war, basic questions about the workings of the Islamic republic remain unanswered.

There is a great deal of speculation about what will happen once the war comes to an end. But while it lasts, and as long as the shadow of the ailing Ayatollah Khomeini continues to loom over Iran, few major changes are expected. When Khomeini dies, a power struggle between factions vying for control is predicted.

▶ Ayatollah Khomeini, who at the age of nearly 80 was a leading figure of the Iranian revolution. Working in exile from Iraq, then Paris, Khomeini was a key inspiration to the opposition. He remained at the forefront of politics in Iran until parliament was elected in 1980, after which, partly due to ill health, he took a back-seat role. However, in his position as supreme interpreter of Islamic law he was still the most powerful figure in the country and his influence remained undiminished. Few politicians progressed without his blessing. His popularity among the masses never waned. Khomeini's insistence on the application of Koranic precepts and his uncompromising stance against other political systems inspired a resurgence of Islamic fundamentalism throughout the Middle East, the reverberations from which will be felt for a long time. His implacable hostility towards Saddam Hussein, ruler of Iraq, was one of the reasons for the outbreak of the war between Iraq and Iran in 1980. Thousands of volunteers rallied to Khomeini's call to take up arms against the enemy.

▲ Shah Muhammad Reza, second ruler of the Pahlavi dynasty. In the eyes of many Iranis, the Shah left Iran as little more than a Western stooge who had misappropriated his country's wealth and undermined its culture for his own ambitions. The rest of his family was accused of having siphoned off national funds to pay for extravagant lifestyles at odds with the values of Irani society. At the time of his departure the Shah was said to have been totally out of touch with his subjects and completely taken off guard by the opposition against him. Once in exile, he found few friends. His last days were spent in Egypt, where President Sadat had defiantly welcomed him. He died in Egypt in 1980.

◀ Young soldiers at the front. The causes of the war which broke out between Iraq and Iran in September 1980 are both historical and contemporary. Territorial disputes and cultural rivalries have existed between the two countries for centuries. In more recent times they squabbled for control of the strategic Shatt al Arab waterway on the Arabian Gulf. The invasion of Iran by Iraq in 1980 came in response to taunts from Tehran calling for the overthrow of the Iraqi regime. The conflict soon developed into a nationalist war. Each side underestimated the other's ability to survive, and thousands died.

▲ In November 1979 student supporters of the Ayatollah Khomeini seized control of the American embassy in Tehran. They held 52 US diplomats hostage for more than a year while they tried to extract a series of demands from the US government. These included the return of the Shah to stand trial and the release of millions of dollars worth of Iranian assets frozen in America. Their refusal to compromise made politicians in the West realize that they were dealing with a serious new force in Iran. The event caused chaos in the American administration and helped to usher out the Carter government. Some of the students spent months painstakingly piecing together shredded documents found in the embassy. These were later published as positive proof of United States interference in the affairs of Iran and other nations in the region. In 1986 Iran had secret contacts with the US in order to secure arms supplies.

Adjustment through violence

An area in turmoil

The Middle East has cultivated a mosaic of political systems within which rival philosophies vie for supremacy. As conflicting forces jostle, the situation becomes more volatile.

External interference in the region has created additional tension. The role of the West in the creation of the state of Israel and the substantial support given to that state by the United States is an enduring source of bitterness which has been transformed into violence. The perceived role of the Western powers in supporting the Shah contributed to the rise of Islamic fundamentalism, which advocates a strict application of Koranic principles in all aspects of life. Western encroachment on the oil-rich Gulf states is a source of resentment among sections of the population.

The role of the Soviet Union in backing states like Syria and Libya serves to keep political rivalries alive between these states and those aligned to the West.

The conflicts are encapsulated in Lebanon, where local rivalries are exploited by outside forces. Syrian soldiers move in and out of Lebanon in support of allied militia such as the Druse and Shia, whom they supply with Soviet weaponry. Christian Lebanese militia use American weaponry supplied by Israel to carry out security operations against Palestinians and Irani-backed Shia in south Lebanon. Funds for other groups trickle in from a variety of sources anxious to promote an ideology or prevent the spread of others. All of this takes place against a background of constantly shifting allegiances.

On a more massive scale there is the Gulf war between Iran and Iraq, now in its seventh year. Its outcome is awaited with trepidation. Victory for Iran would certainly mean a boost for fundamentalism and possibly territorial encroachment by Iran into neighbouring states.

The support given to Iraq by the Gulf monarchies is one way of trying to stem the tide of the Islamic revolution. Support given to Iran by Syria and Libya underlines local rivalries.

Reactions among the population

The advent of the Iranian revolution has caused a revision of ideas among sections of the population in most countries. Young people in particular seem to draw strength from reasserting their religion and culture as a challenge to pro-foreign tendencies of previous generations. For the moment they have no objection to returning to traditional dress and falling in line with modes of behaviour which their parents probably fought to do away with. But their attitude is not universal; many others feel that their freedom will become unbearably restricted should the traditionalists gain the upper hand. A general feeling of disenchantment with Western ideas has encouraged some radical rethinking at many levels.

Economic factors

The changing economic fortunes of the region have also influenced the shaping of attitudes. The gap between rich and poor is still tremendous and, as society has become more concerned with material wealth, the contrast is more painful. Falling back on traditional values is one obvious way in which the 'have-nots' try to cope. The quality of life is gradually improving for most people, but recession has set things back. There is still great economic potential in the area. Much depends on how it is exploited and how its rewards are distributed.

◀ As the violence of Middle Eastern politics spilled out into other areas in the form of terrorism against Western targets, the victim nations mustered their forces to combat the threat. When the bombings and hijackings increased, the pressure for decisive action mounted. The Reagan administration in the US selected a scapegoat in the person of Libya's maverick leader, Colonel Gaddafi, a known supporter of terrorist action. In April 1986 American war planes undertook a bombing raid on Libya. Many innocent people were killed in this largely symbolic action which did little to quash terrorism and a lot to reinforce hostility against the uneven policy of the US.

▼ Forty years after the establishment of the state of Israel in Palestine, the violence continues. Israeli society has been divided on the question of the right of the Palestinians to a homeland. The most moderate elements now campaign for a Palestinian state. The most extreme, such as these armed settlers, are ready to take the law into their own hands to keep the Arabs off land which they consider to be theirs by biblical right. On the Arab side, attitudes are equally divided. Moderates who seek compromise can run the risk of being liquidated by extremists who refuse anything other than the elimination of Israel. It is acknowledged that until the Palestinian problem is solved, there cannot be peace in the Middle East.

◀ Shia militiamen in South Lebanon. Historically the Shia have been underdogs to the Islamic Sunni majority. In South Lebanon their community suffered deprivation at every level. Their situation deteriorated when they became caught in border cross-fire between Israel and the PLO. They evacuated in their thousands to the slums of Beirut, where they nursed resentment. The upsurge of Shiism through the Islamic revolution changed their position. With Iranian support they were trained, equipped and transformed into an uncompromising political and religious force. Their fighters derive strength from the Shia belief in martyrdom. They see themselves as engaged in a 'holy war' against alien forces. Extremist Shia attacked Western targets in Beirut and seized hostages. Their actions have inspired Shia groups in other countries where the desire to impose fundamentalist ideals gains ground.

▼ Damage in Beirut caused by fighting in the Lebanese civil war which started in 1975. The war in Lebanon has come to represent a microcosm of the many conflicts dividing the region. It broke out because of internal tensions aggravated by the growing military presence of Lebanon's Palestinian refugees. It soon evolved into a complex struggle between opposing sectarian, social, political and ideological forces. Outsiders, eager to tip the balance, were drawn in: Syria, Iran and Israel became actively embroiled. The UN and temporary peacekeeping forces from Britain, France, Italy and the US failed to ameliorate the situation. Life has inevitably deteriorated for the majority of innocent Lebanese. This gruesome theatre of war being played out in their country is, in part, the legacy of historical events in the Middle East.

The economy

Development of the oil industry

The discovery of oil in the Middle East transformed a largely unproductive desert area into one of the wealthiest regions in the world.

The first oil finds were uncovered in the early twentieth century. Major explorations took place at the beginning of the 1930s. Saudi Arabia, Iraq, Iran, Kuwait, Qatar and the United Arab Emirates all granted exploration rights and concessions to foreign oil companies. The first oil exports were around 1934–35.

Production was stepped up after the Second World War. At this time the foreign oil companies held almost total control of oil production and kept a major share of the profits. It was not until the 1960s that the oil producers made a move to play a role in running the oil industry, and not until the early 1970s that they eventually achieved

participation. By the late 1970s they were able to assume real control over oil extraction.

Between late 1973 and early 1974 the price of oil was increased almost four-fold. It went up several times after that and the sudden increase brought billions of dollars flooding into the producing countries. Money was channelled into new industries and development programmes. A banking and investment sector was created. Some of the money was diverted into projects in poorer countries in the region in order to encourage economic growth in the area as a whole.

Developing new industries

The oil producers also saw the wisdom of developing new industries of their own. Petrochemical production is one such industry which uses the oil as a starting material to make chemicals. In Saudi Arabia comprehensive industrial complexes were built at Jubail on the Gulf coast and Yanbo on the Red Sea. These include steel mills, fertilizer and petrochemical plants and other oil-related industries.

Recession

In the early 1980s the price of oil began to drop as production in other areas of the world picked up and alternative energy sources, including nuclear power stations, became available. As revenues decreased the

Middle East entered a period of recession which experts predict will endure into the 1990s. Many projects were cut back as governments struggled to meet their budget deficits. The effect on the region was considerable. Thousands of people working in the Gulf had to return to countries where there were already job shortages.

Mouths to feed

Egypt, Jordan, Lebanon and the occupied West Bank of Palestine, whose economies had come to depend on remissions sent from workers in the Gulf, have been hard hit by the loss of income. These are among the most densely-populated countries and they do not have enough industrial development to absorb their work-force. Egypt and Syria have some oil, Jordan has a little and Lebanon has none at all. They have concentrated more on building up their agricultural industry.

Agriculture

Throughout the Middle East food production has high priority. The population of the region is expanding and imported supplies are expensive. Only about 10 per cent of the land is cultivated. Steps are being taken to redevelop lost arable lands. New farming methods are being tested and ambitious irrigation systems are being built. These hold much promise for the future.

▲ In contrast to the new industries based on oil, Egypt and Syria have a centuries-old textile industry. This is a modern spinning and weaving mill in Egypt. The world cotton market is generally rather unstable and there is always talk about turning the land over to food production. Syria has adopted this policy in some areas.

▲ Oil is not simply a source of fuel. It contains (or can be converted into) chemical compounds which cannot be conveniently produced any other way. This plant in Qatar uses local oil to produce fertilizer needed for the developing agricultural industry. Many oil-producing states have invested in petrochemical processing plants, which in turn have given rise to secondary industries manufacturing products like plastics and paint additives.

▶ Oil wells in the Qatar desert with associated gas burning off in huge flares. Though they are undeniably spectacular, these flares are a waste of a precious resource. Increasingly the gases produced with petroleum are being used locally as fuel or are compressed and exported. Qatar is also known to have large reserves of natural gas which until now have not been exploited. Funds for the development of this valuable resource are scarce at present and Qatar faces a dilemma on how best to market the gas once it is in a position to start production.

◀ In a number of countries encouraging results have been obtained from experimental agricultural programmes. Here cucumbers are being grown hydroponically in a temperature-controlled greenhouse in Abu Dhabi. The plants are grown in plastic tubes without soil. Plant food dissolved in water is pumped through the tubes. Crops using this method can often be harvested within weeks of planting. Other agricultural innovations include dairy farming, previously unknown in the Gulf area, and chicken rearing. A major success story has been Saudi Arabia's wheat programme. In the past the country depended on imports, now there are surpluses and even exports.

The cities

No room for growth

The older cities, which include some of the most ancient in the world, do not have the scope to handle the expanding population and the influx of new people coming in search of work. There is a lack of housing, and basic services are inadequate. Over-population has caused pressure at many levels and some areas have fallen into slums. Families move to the city looking for well-paid jobs. Instead, they may end up living in poverty, several to a room. Because the old cities were not designed to cater for motorized transport, traffic congestion is a major problem and public transport systems have been difficult to devise. Vehicle-related pollution is an additional problem.

Lack of planning

In the modern cities of the Gulf space is more abundant and there is room for expansion. But these cities were the result of rapid development brought about by oil wealth, when there was not enough time for adequate planning. Buildings were erected in haste, with little thought for practicality or design. Within a matter of years, strips of bare desert were filled with towering skyscrapers or straggling residential complexes. Speed and convenience were the aim and the results were sometimes ugly and shabby.

Sadly, where old buildings existed, these were too often destroyed and replaced by characterless office blocks. Speculation in new office or apartment space was rife, but the buildings sometimes stood empty because rents were too high or the demand for offices too low. When recession hit the Gulf area in the mid-1980s rents came down, but so did the demand. It will take time for things to finally stabilize.

Improvements under way

Today, more thought and effort are being put into improving the cities, old and new. Parts of ancient Cairo are intended for restoration; there are moves to resuscitate areas of Damascus now in disrepair; and there are ambitious plans for ancient Sana'a in Yemen. New housing areas are being built on the fringes of some of the older cities to relieve the pressure there.

In the Gulf cities a great deal more thought is being given to zoning and planning and to the type of architecture used in public building schemes. Integrated landscape projects, parks and leisure areas have been designed and museums and cultural centres are being built. Older parts of the cities are being renovated and rehabilitated. Though recession has led to the halting of many projects, a commitment to improve the quality of city life remains. Public works programmes and town and city planning schedules continue apace.

◀ Modernization has transformed the face of commerce in most cities. Here in Kuwait the traditional *souq* is rivalled by a glittering shopping mall with a wide variety of shops. In the new *'supersouq'* food markets, goods are sold from all over the world: New Zealand lamb, English apples and gourmet French cheeses, as well as every sort of packed or canned food. There is no more bargaining over prices. Shopping is quick and easy, but may be a lot more impersonal.

▶ The old market area or *souq* of the Iranian city of Isfahan. Though the city has been modernized, a flourishing *souq* still survives in the centre of the old town. Here life appears to have changed little over the centuries. Almost everything can be bought, from sheepskins to sugar, jugs to jewellery, pipes to pomegranates. In their tiny open-fronted shops merchants haggle with customers over the price of goods, and when agreement is reached it is often sealed with a cup of coffee supplied by the shopkeeper. The old *souqs* were large and well organized into different sectors for the various goods. They had inns, restaurants and even public baths.

◀ The streets of Cairo, Egypt's capital city. Originally founded a thousand years ago as a spacious city on the Nile delta, it later had very little room in which to grow. Now it is choking with a population of over ten million. Cairo is a city literally bursting at the seams. The streets are always crowded. The roads are jammed with traffic. Many buildings are crumbling with age and neglect. Everything is in short supply. Yet despite all the problems, Cairo is a warm, vibrant city, steeped in history. It has its own faded beauty.

▶ The sprawling city of Jeddah. Jeddah's growth was so rapid that for a time the basic infrastructure was unable to cope with the demand. Massive investments have been made in the city's development and in improving its appearance. Already sections of the modern city have been rebuilt, while the remaining areas of the old city have been attractively restored. Tree planting and landscaping schemes have been implemented to upgrade several areas, especially the sea-front Corniche. By night, with its glittering lights, this assumes a fairy-tale appearance.

Traditional lifestyles

▼ Muslims must pray five specified times a day, starting at sunrise and finishing late in the evening. They go to the mosque, the Muslim place of worship, when they can; but this is not necessary. At the appointed hours it is therefore quite common to see desert herdsmen or farmers in their field stop and unroll a prayer rug or simply kneel down in a quiet spot, to perform sacred rites. They always pray facing Mecca, kneeling and touching the ground with their foreheads in submission to Allah. The Muslim holy day is Friday.

Bedouin tenacity

Migration to the cities in search of work has been widespread, but it has not always brought the rewards it promised. There are still many who prefer the old way of life.

For some people in Jordan, Syria, Iran, Israel and the Arabian peninsula the traditional way of life is nomadic. All the governments in the Middle East have at some stage made it policy to encourage the nomads to settle. Thousands have agreed, but many have resisted.

These people, known as bedouin, roam the deserts with their herds in search of forage. They are replacing their camels with sheep and goats and some use motorized transport for themselves and their animals. Several families may pool their resources to buy a truck which is used for transport to pasture. This has the benefit of getting the animals to short-lived forage quickly. Also, it allows the bedouin to bring their animals to market according to the demand for meat.

In recent times the bedouin were accused of overgrazing land and turning potential pasture into desert. In fact, they are well aware of the problems of over-grazing and since ancient times have used even the poorest lands to advantage. During grazing the bedouin do not always acknowledge the restrictions of national boundaries. This has sometimes caused them trouble with the authorities.

Role of the family

In many ways the bedouin lifestyle has changed little for centuries. All members of the family have a working role. The women, perhaps, work the hardest since they are partly responsible for grazing and must organize fuel collection, cooking and child care, as well as putting together their tent homes and furnishings. The primary concern of the men is protection of the family and herd, and marketing the animals. Children work alongside their parents.

The problem of schooling has encouraged some bedouin to assume a semi-settled lifestyle in proximity to a township. Some governments provide transport so that children can be picked up for school. Otherwise, they receive limited instruction from anyone who is capable from among their group.

Farming communities

Among the settled farming people, agricultural tasks normally involve the whole family. Children work on the land before and after school. Women are expected to perform farmwork as well as household duties. It is a hard existence.

Some of the farming methods are very outdated, and the prices fetched are often barely enough to keep the family going. New methods cost money and are often viewed with suspicion. Government attempts to introduce collective farming are usually rejected.

Modern developments have, by and large, left these people behind. Their houses are usually single-storey dwellings of mudbrick or concrete, sometimes comprising only one room, with an earthenware fireplace in a corner or just outside the door. In many cases water is collected from a well. There is little furniture.

The style of dress has also changed little over the years. Though some of the men may now have adopted trousers, it is still common to see them in the full-length, long-sleeved gowns known variously as *thobes* or *dishdashas*. At night and in colder weather, a heavy sleeveless coat known as an *abbaya* is worn. A head-covering known as a *kefiyya* is held in place by a twisted band called an *agal*. The women wear full-length, long-sleeved dresses, often very colourful, and some kind of veil or head-covering. Like their bedouin peers, the women like to invest in gold jewellery, if they have the means. In some communities, especially the Palestinian one, the women take great pride in their embroidery skills which are primarily displayed on their own everyday clothes. Girls learn such skills at an early age. Boys are generally expected to work alongside their fathers.

◄ These unusual pointed dwellings and grain silos near Aleppo in northern Syria are built in a way that has remained unchanged for centuries. It is known that houses were being built in the Middle East around 9000 years ago. The earliest were primitive mounds, but later mud bricks were used. Over the years the dwellings became more sophisticated, even being built on two storeys. Sometimes the bricks were left unbaked, as in southern Iraq. Elsewhere they were mixed with straw and baked, as in Egypt. Though these bricks contain properties better suited to the climate, concrete is now more popular, being equated with modernism and progress.

► Bedouin women in front of their home in Qatar. Bedouin tents are made from woven strips of camel or goat hair, about 60 centimetres wide and between 1½ and 4 metres long. These are stitched together to form the main body of the tent, which is often very large. This is supported by three to five central poles and smaller poles for the sides. The tent is warm and waterproof in winter. In summer, with the side flaps raised for ventilation, it provides protection from the sun. Inside, other strips are sewn together as walls. There is always one room with a fireplace scooped out of the ground. Here the men sit talking and brewing coffee on a charcoal fire. The women usually keep to the smaller rooms with the family. There is no furniture, only colourful woven rugs and cushions. When not in use these are stacked away with the bedding.

◄ A water buffalo provides the power to operate this old-fashioned pump which supplies water to irrigate the field. Though some of the parts are now made of metal, wooden pumps of the same basic design have been used in Egypt for thousands of years. The animal is blindfolded so that it does not become dizzy as it plods round its circular path. Mechanized or electric water pumps are much more efficient but most farmers are too poor to buy and install them. Today's hand-made wooden tools look just like those in ancient wall drawings. It it still common to see farmers, wearing the long blue *gallabeya*, walking behind a pair of oxen pulling a wooden plough of ancient design. Many traditional agricultural techniques survive in the Middle East.

The family

The role of the family

Although there is a shift towards the nuclear family, the extended family system prevails. Sometimes three or more generations live together. In the Gulf countries, among affluent families, they share 'compounds' comprising a number of houses. In the cities, where lack of space would preclude this, families try to stay in close proximity and visit each other often.

Families still tend to be large. In poor countries like Egypt where there is an enormous population, birth control is unofficially encouraged. The role of grandparents, and even aunts and uncles, in the care and education of the children has always been important. Older children play a part in looking after younger siblings.

Where society has become more industrialized or the people are better off, children are less involved in the work-force than before and can enjoy childhood and adolescence. There is a new emphasis on providing leisure facilities for the young.

Social taboos in courtship

People tend to marry young and the family plays a role in the choice of partner. The system of arranged marriages still exists, though it may have become more subtle. Among traditional rural groups the families may have committed their children when they were small. Otherwise, candidates are put forward as adolescence approaches. Even in the cities and among the more educated groups, it is common for friends or relatives to play matchmaker by suggesting suitable partners. It is not common for a couple to meet by chance or on their own initiative. It is normal practice for them to be introduced to each other in the presence of the family.

The family remains closely involved in the process of courtship. There is almost always a chaperone present when a couple meets.

▲ Outings, like this one in Kuwait, are a popular way of spending time as a family. In the Gulf area and Saudi Arabia women are still expected to veil in public. This custom is associated with Islam, but it pre-dates it. It was relatively unusual in the Prophet's time and became more widespread after the Turkish conquest. There have always been women who refused to wear the veil, but it became a subject of major controversy in the early part of this century when it came to be regarded as a symbol of repression. The ex-Shah of Iran ordered women to remove the veil. His opponents adopted it as a symbol of defiance. Supporters of the Islamic movement elsewhere followed suit. Pressure to return to the veil or head-covering is increasing.

▼ The social life of people in the Middle East is still family oriented. Children are greatly loved and are included in most activities, even evening outings to restaurants or public places. There is a lot of respect for the older generation. The role of the grandparents in the day-to-day care of children is very valuable, especially if the mother works. Grandmothers usually take charge when a new baby comes along; the mothers are still encouraged to take a 40-day rest period. In theory society in the Middle East is patriarchal, but in practice the women control a great deal from behind the scenes. They are, nevertheless, excluded from many events and spend a great deal of time segregated with other women.

The idea of the two going out alone together is still frowned upon in all but the most liberal of households. In the Gulf area it is practically unheard of.

Family law

A woman's rights within the Islamic system are generally misunderstood by outsiders. According to the Koran, a woman should lay down terms and conditions for her marriage and has as much right to ask for a divorce as her husband as long as this is provided for in her marriage contract. A couple sign the marriage contract in the presence of a *shaikh* (religious leader), after which they are officially man and wife. Wedding celebrations are purely festive. At the time of the marriage the wife is given a dowry by her husband. This gift becomes her property; she keeps it if she is widowed or divorced. A woman's property is hers exclusively; she can dispose of it as she wishes. The right of the man to divorce is subject to several conditions. Unfortunately not everybody is aware of the law. It takes a determined woman to tackle the male-dominated legal system and get her rights. Divorce is, on the whole, easier for the man and it is the father, not the mother, who gets custody of the children after a certain age.

Under Islamic law a man is allowed to have up to four wives at once. It is stressed that he must provide for them all and treat them all equally. This originates from a time when women were entirely dependent on men. It was seen by the Prophet Muhammad as a way of taking care of widows and orphans. Nowadays, polygamy is rare, for economic, if for no other reason.

Women in the work-force

Economic factors have played a role in encouraging women to join the work-force. According to the law in most countries there is no discrimination against women in pay or employment. Women are allowed maternity leave while their jobs are kept open for them. After she returns the mother has an extra hour off to feed her child. As more and more women have officially entered the work-force in recent years, they have taken giant steps towards asserting their rights.

▲ In the rural areas all members of the family participate in the work-force. Children automatically help out, but some are placed in paid employment at an early age to help maintain the rest of the family. Their jobs include agricultural labouring and street vending. Where the opportunity arises, a girl might be placed in domestic service. In city and countryside alike too many children still lose their education because they become wage earners. In some cases all the family will work to provide an education for the oldest or the brightest child, who would help out financially once qualified.

▼ Policewomen operating in the control room of the Omani police force. In many parts of the Middle East the women took an active role in the struggle for national independence. They were not willing to go back to a subservient role once the struggle was over. In Iraq, Syria, Israel, Jordan, Lebanon and Egypt women are employed at all levels including the army and police force. This trend is now reaching the Gulf, though the number of professions open to women is still limited. There are some state-run nurseries to take care of children while their parents work. Usually, however, other members of the family step in.

The arts past and present

Love of poetry

Poetry was the earliest art to flourish. Because people were illiterate the verses were passed on by word of mouth and embellished as they went. Later they were collected and copied.

Arabic and Persian languages are rich in meaning. Some words, such as those used in praise of Allah, have hundreds of forms. Subtleties of meaning are used for poetic effect. Poetry still plays an important role in the culture of the Middle East and recitations still attract crowds.

Legendary figures emerged from the poetic tradition including the Sumerian hero Gilgamesh whose deeds were copied on cuneiform tables. Later came the black knight Antar whose prowess in war and love for Lady Abla are now classic. More famous are the characters from *One Thousand and One Nights*, cruel king Shahriyar, and clever Shahrazad whose nightly tales saved her from execution.

As writing developed, so did the art of calligraphy. It takes the elaborate shapes of the Arabic alphabet and combines them into designs. This started with the copying of the Koran and developed into five schools.

Abstract art

Traditional art of the Middle East symbolizes the role of Islam in daily life. Buildings, weapons and even utensils were decorated with patterns or motifs which reflected the faith of those who produced them. The Islamic religion discouraged any form of representational art, based on Muhammad's doctrine that only Allah can create life. Instead there was calligraphy and arabesques – complicated floral or geometric patterns.

These had an impact on modern Western painters and helped to inspire the early schools of modern art. In turn the new movements influenced would-be artists in the Middle East where the concept of studio art was new. Initially inhibited by European styles, the artists gradually developed their own distinctive school.

The shapes and patterns adopted by modern artists have been used for centuries in carpet weaving, an art in which the Persians excelled. They also pioneered the art of the book, producing fine miniature paintings based on stories in the Koran or other famous tales. They were assembled in tooled leather bindings – art pieces in themselves.

▲ Islamic architecture expresses beauty and common sense. High ceilings, small windows and thick walls provide a cool interior even in the hottest weather. Buildings face inwards to an open courtyard with a fountain. The windows are set back behind carved shades which give protection from the sun and allow those inside to look out without being seen. Domes, arches and decorative elements like friezes and ceramics add key aesthetic touches.

◀ A design in the shape of a pear by Hashem al-Khattat. This work comprises sayings from the Koran, written in two different scripts. The body of the pear and its leaves are in Thuluth script; underneath the lines are in Nashki. It is part of the calligrapher's skill that every line is part of the text, even those which appear at first sight to be outlines.

▶ A craftsman displays his jewellery. The bedouins kept few possessions but jewellery was one way in which wealth could be conveniently invested. It used to be the custom for a woman to receive jewellery as part of her dowry from her husband. Necklaces, bracelets, anklets, pendants, earrings, rings and heavy embossed belts were decorated with semi-precious stones or delicate filigree work, bells and other trinkets. Amulets, mainly in the form of an eye or hand, were worn to bring good luck. Styles of jewellery have changed but the tradition of investing in it continues. Other crafts produced in the Middle East include weaving, basketry, embroidery, metal-engraving, woodcarving, glass-making and ceramics. In some countries the governments have started schemes to keep these crafts alive, but they are in danger of becoming extinct.

◀ A play on stage in Qatar. Despite conservative opposition to the idea of theatre, it is now being officially encouraged in some Gulf states. The theatre movement in the Arab world began in Egypt and Lebanon around the turn of the century and gathered force with Arab nationalism in the 1920s. The leaders saw it as an effective way of getting their point across. For this same reason it became popular in Syria and Iraq during the fight for independence in the 1940s. During the next two decades it flourished, but its liberal political views caused some leaders to view it less favourably. Today, theatre is subject to strict censorship laws. The performing arts are still not really accepted in the Gulf area but support is given to traditional folk groups in an effort to keep alive ancient songs and dances of the region.

35

Food and entertainment

The tradition of hospitality

Food and social eating are of almost ritual importance in the Middle East. Great emphasis is placed on hospitality. If a bedouin came across a stranger in the desert it would be a matter of honour to take the stranger home to a feast. Today in the cities it is still the custom to honour guests by inviting them home. Food is always prepared in excess.

Eating is a social pastime. Families visit each other for elaborate meals. People go to restaurants in groups. Meals are long and leisurely. Children are included, even at night.

Range of foods

Though the countries of the Middle East are in some ways diverse, food is a great uniter. The recipes cover a wide range, and many are highly imaginative. They make maximum use of often limited ingredients blended with herbs and spices. Some of the basic recipes originated with the Turks during their long occupation of the area. They were embellished as time went on.

Lamb is consumed in vast quantities. A traditional favourite is *kharouf mahshi*, whole baked lamb stuffed with rice and nuts and flavoured with spices. In the coastal regions there is a variety of fish dishes. In the Gulf area stuffed baked fish is popular. Before the days of airfreight and refrigerators, bread, rice and dates were the staples of the Arabian peninsula.

A variety of vegetarian dishes complement the meat plates in the milder coastal areas where ingredients are plentiful. Among the poor, appetizing meals are made from beans, lentils, chick peas and other nourishing protein-containing pulses are eaten. Yoghurt is a popular side dish. Fruit is eaten in quantity.

Coffee is favourite

No meal is complete without coffee. This is usually 'Turkish' coffee, a strong concentrated mixture served in tiny cups. Arabic coffee, a thin, bitter liquid mixed with cardomom, was traditionally brewed by the bedouin over their campfires. Nowadays in the cities it is served from vacuum flasks. One cannot go anywhere in the Middle East without being offered coffee.

Music and dance

Music plays an important part in daily life. There is rarely a coffee house or taxi that does not have a cassette recorder or radio blaring music continuously. A good heartrending ballad can almost stop the traffic.

The belly dance is a form of musical entertainment which is unique to the Middle East. This requires a great deal of strenuous movement on the part of the women who perform it and they must be very physically fit.

▲ The equivalent to hors d'oeuvres in the Middle East is *mezza*, a large variety of savoury appetizers. A favourite is *hommos*, chick peas blended with garlic, lemon and *tahini* (a creamy paste made from crushed sesame seeds). *Kibbe nayyeh* is raw lamb, finely minced and mixed with crushed wheat, onions and spices. Cooked *kibbe*, served as hollow balls, is made from the same ingredients. There are bean dishes, salads and pastries. Most dishes are eaten with a scoop of bread torn from flat Arabic loaves.

◀ A video library. Until recently, in many countries of the Middle East, cinema was popular. Now television, and especially the video, have begun to take over and video libraries have opened everywhere. They stock both Western and Arabic films. The latter are made mainly in Egypt which, until a few years ago, had one of the world's largest film industries. High production costs and distribution problems have led to cutbacks in the Egyptian cinema, but the new video market has helped to keep the industry going.

► A traditional orchestra. Middle Eastern music has a special sound and beat. It is intricate in rhythm and rather ritualized in form. To Western ears it may sound melancholy and out of tune. Some of the instruments used in a traditional orchestra have changed little over the centuries. They are in fact the forerunners to a number of Western instruments. They include the *qunun* (zither), the *oud* (lute), the *nay* (flute), the *riqq* (tambourine), *tablah* (drum) as well as the violin and sometimes the cello and accordian. When solo singers perform with the orchestra there is a great deal of improvisation between them which requires a skill much appreciated by the audience. A single 'song' may last over half an hour. Some orchestras are accompanied by a full choir. Audience participation in the form of clapping and cheering is encouraged.

◄ The traditional meal celebrated during Ramadan, the ninth month of the Muslim year. Throughout the holy month of Ramadan the faithful are required to practise self-sacrifice through fasting and prayer. Nothing should be eaten or drunk between sunrise and sunset during this period. Because Islam follows a lunar calendar, Ramadan falls at different times each year. The fast is especially difficult during the hot summer months. At sunset the whole family participates together in the one meal of the day. Friends and relatives may come over to eat and the meal assumes a rather festive atmosphere. Special foods and sweets are prepared which are particularly nourishing in order to keep people going during the next day. At the end of Ramadan there is a celebratory feast.

◄ Drinking alcohol is forbidden by Islam. Coffee is the favourite social drink. It would be an insult not to offer coffee and an insult to refuse it. Coffee shops or *qahwa* are found throughout the Middle East. They are usually unadorned cafes where men go to talk and smoke a hubble-bubble pipe or *nargeela*. They are the nearest equivalent to the bars found in Western countries. Tea is also drunk in quantity. It is served in small, delicate glass cups and is usually strong and very sweet. Such is the tradition of hospitality in the area that a shop-keeper will often settle the account by offering his client tea, coffee or a cold drink upon conclusion of purchases.

37

Schools and education

Koranic education

The Prophet Muhammad told the people to 'seek knowledge from the cradle to the grave', but it was a long time before schools were established.

Education was left to the parents. At first the only 'textbook' was the Koran, which was memorized. Eventually a system of private tutors developed. Some of these formed groups for students which became known as *kuttab*. These were the first Islamic elementary schools. Apart from the Koran, simple mathematics and some poetry were taught. This system has prevailed until today in some remote areas where small children are taught to read and write, working from the Koran.

First steps in higher education

The founding of the Al-Azhar in Cairo in 973, the oldest university in the world, heralded a more systematic approach to higher education. Gradually, throughout the Islamic empire the establishment of colleges or *madrasahs* became more widespread. Teachers were paid by the state. Students received free tuition and sometimes board and lodging. The colleges became important centres of learning.

Western influence

The growth of modern education has been uneven. It started primarily in Egypt in the first half of the nineteenth century. Muhammad Ali, the ruler of Egypt, opened state secondary schools with foreign instructors, against opposition from the theologians. He also founded colleges of medicine and engineering and sent students to Europe for training.

Meanwhile in Syria and Lebanon Muhammad Ali's son, Ibrahim, started a public education system. Catholic and Protestant missionaries also opened schools which eventually developed into important institutions, such as the American University of Beirut which was founded in 1866. This became one of the most influential universities in the Middle East. The first girls' schools began in Lebanon in the 1870s. Other countries soon followed suit.

For a long time the Gulf countries remained cut off from these developments. Educational facilities were virtually non-existent until the beginning of the twentieth century. Since then, every effort has gone into providing education at all levels.

Compulsory education

Today elementary schooling is compulsory in many countries, though the law is not always strictly observed. Since the mid-1950s emphasis has been given to secondary and higher education. There are over 40 universities in the region, with new ones planned. There is also special emphasis on providing technical and vocational training facilities. It is hoped that eventually much of the skilled labour will be provided locally.

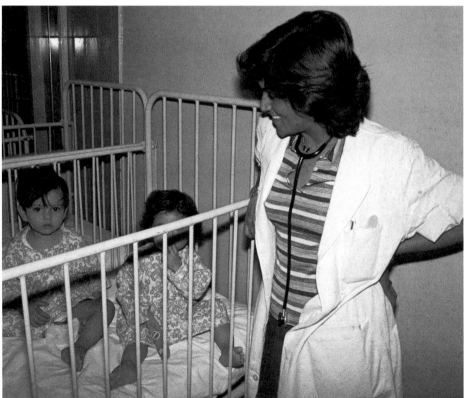

▲ A doctor at work in Kuwait. When other professions were denied to women in the Middle East, nursing was accepted. For a long time it was regarded as the only road to higher education. Nowadays female enrolment in some university faculties sometimes exceeds that of men, and the women are found to be the most serious students. In the Gulf area and Iran education is strictly segregated.

Here also, opportunities to mix at a professional level are limited so girls tend to choose subjects which will allow them to work. Medicine is still popular, along with teaching, journalism and, since the establishment of women's banks, finance. Elsewhere in the region there is co-education and women enter most professions. Here, pay and work opportunities are on a par with men.

▲ In the Gulf area education at the tertiary level has received priority in recent years. More than a dozen new universities have opened. These cater to undergraduates in a range of faculties but they still lack facilities for post-graduate work. Where possible, teaching is in Arabic but English is widely used for medical, science and engineering subjects. Many professors are from other Arab countries or from the West. Critics of the new universities complain that the curricula do not take into consideration the developmental needs of the area. Educational planners trying to deal with the problem are seeking greater co-operation between education ministries to co-ordinate programmes.

▲ A girls' primary school in Jeddah, Saudi Arabia. Most countries lay down a minimum of six years of schooling for girls and nine years for boys. In some of the poor countries, such as Egypt and Syria, parents cannot afford to keep their children in school. Although tuition is free, they do not have money to pay for uniforms and books. Sometimes children are forced to leave school so that they can work to help maintain their families. Some manage with part-time jobs.

The schools themselves have problems. In some countries the classrooms are very overcrowded, and basic materials are in short supply. In others, especially the Gulf, money and space is not a problem but there is a shortage of teachers. Many teachers working there are Egyptians who find the pay and conditions are better than at home. Despite the difficulties, attendance rates are climbing and there is progress. The commitment to education is growing.

▶ A class of adults learning to read and write in Damascus, Syria. Compulsory education is relatively new and is still not always enforced. There are therefore many adults who are illiterate. In most countries there are adult literacy programmes to teach the basic reading and writing skills. Because of the pressures of working and bringing up a family, these classes are often not well attended. A few years ago, Iraq took a drastic step of making adult literacy classes compulsory for those between the ages of 15 and 45. Failure to attend meant prosecution. In other countries campaigns are launched on a periodic basis to try to eradicate the problem, but progress is slow.

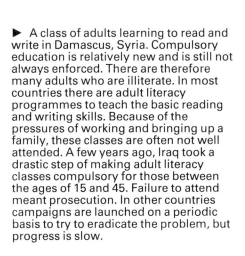

Sport and leisure

The old and the new

The idea of competitive sport is a relatively new one in the Middle East. Races for camels and horses have been held among the bedouin for centuries. Hunting and falconry were serious occupations. But it was only at the turn of this century that competitive sport as it is known in the West was adopted.

Organized sporting activities were introduced in the curricula of the Christian missionary colleges in the area. Track and field athletics, tennis and swimming were all included. With the influx of soldiers into the area during the First World War, other sports, particularly soccer, became more familiar.

A passion for soccer

Soccer was first adopted by the Egyptians for whom it is now a national passion. Egyptian soccer teams took part in the World Cup as early as the 1920s.

Football is the most popular sport in the region, followed by basketball, volleyball, weightlifting, swimming, tennis and squash. Tennis has been played in the area for several decades and a number of countries have taken part in international contests like Wimbledon.

Squash is new, but it has caught on quickly. In the Gulf states air-conditioned courts make it one of the few all-year-round sports. Other gym sports are gaining momentum for the same reason.

Water sports and recreation

Although there are millions of swimmers, competitive swimming is another recent innovation. The Egyptians have been competing internationally for some time. They have a good reputation in long-distance events and some records to their credit.

In the coastal regions people have taken up sailing and, more recently, water-skiing and wind-surfing.

Golf is another popular innovation. There have been courses in Egypt and Lebanon since the 1940s; now it is catching on in the other countries including Saudi Arabia. Here the courses are rough and sandy and the balls are bright red to make them easy to spot.

For such a hot dry climate perhaps the strangest sport of all is ice-skating which was introduced into the Gulf countries a few years ago. In the mountains of Syria, Lebanon and Iran snow-skiing is enjoyed by the wealthy.

Most governments try to encourage sport and some invest heavily in sporting facilities, especially for the young. Until now sport has remained primarily a preoccupation of the men.

◀ Backgammon may not be as energetic as other games, but the competitive spirit can be just as fierce. It has been played in the Middle East for at least 5000 years, and is known there as *tawle*. It is a widespread leisure pastime among the men. They play for hours at a time, either at home or in local coffee shops. It is a basic day-to-day game, played with simple boards and equipment. This contrasts markedly with the lavish kits and complicated instructions which appeared in the West when the game became popular there.

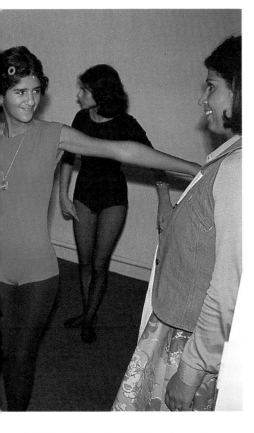

▲ Throughout the Gulf region, where attitudes are very conservative, comprehensive leisure centres have been created where women and children enjoy sport and relax, out of view from the general public. These centres include swimming pools, refreshment and amusement areas. They may also have sports facilities for the men, which are segregated from the family area. Elsewhere in the region, trips to the beach or public parks are very much a family affair.

◀ Soccer match in Bahrain. Soccer is the most popular spectator sport throughout the Middle East. The richer countries have put a lot of money and effort into improving their teams. New stadiums have been built, most of them equipped with powerful floodlights so that games can be played in the cool of the evening. Famous overseas players have worked there as trainers and managers to help develop the national teams. Some of these teams now participate in the World Cup and other international competitions. There are thousands of amateur players too. Every state has its own league.

▶ A camel race in Saudi Arabia. Informal camel racing has been part of desert life for centuries. These days the sport also has its professional side. Races usually take place on tracks outside the main cities in the late afternoon. Gambling is forbidden by Islamic law, but that does not reduce the excitement. Horse racing has recently started in the Gulf. The annual King's Cup race in Saudi Arabia has great pomp and formality.

▲ Wrestling is one of the oldest sports in the Middle East. Engravings depicting wrestlers from Pharaonic times have been found in Egypt. Iran is perhaps foremost in wrestling. Its teams have been successful in many international competitions and have brought home Olympic medals. The area has also produced several world-class weight-lifters. In recent years, a number of athletes have come to prominence and have participated internationally. Many Gulf teenagers are fascinated by cars; some have ambitions to be race drivers.

Reference

Countries of the Middle East

Bahrain
Independent sheikhdom since 1971; previously in exclusive treaty relations with Britain.
Area: 684.9 square kms
Population: 368 908* (1982)
Capital: Manama

Egypt
Republic since 1953; previously an independent kingdom.
Area: 997 738.5 square kms
Population: 45 915 000* (1983)
Capital: Cairo

Iran
Islamic republic since overthrow of the Shah in 1979; previously an absolute monarchy.
Area: 1 648 000 square kms
Population: 43 414 000* (1984)
Capital: Tehran

Iraq
Independent republic since 1958; previously a monarchy.
Area: 438 317 square kms
Population: 14 110 425* (1982)
Capital: Baghdad

Israel
Independent republic since 1948.
Area: 21 946 square kms
Population: 4 037 620 (1983)
Population under occupation:
1 279 000 (1983)
Capital: Jerusalem

Jordan
Independent kingdom since 1946; previously British mandated territory of Transjordan.
Area: 89 206 square kms (E. Bank)
97 740 sq kms (with occupied W. Bank)
Population: 3 247 000** (1983)
E. Bank: 2 495 300 (1983)
Capital: Amman

Kuwait
Independent sheikhdom since 1961; previously in exclusive treaty relations with Britain since 1899.
Area: 17 818 square kms
Population: 1 709 859* (1985)
Capital: Kuwait City

Lebanon
Independent republic since 1946; formerly French mandated territory.
Area: 10 452 square kms
Population: 2 644 000** (1984)
Capital: Beirut

Oman
Independent sultanate.
Area: 300 000 square kms
Population: 2 000 000 (1985)
Capital: Muscat

Qatar
Independent sheikhdom, 1971.
Area: 11 437 square kms
Population: 270 000* (1985)
Capital: Doha

Saudi Arabia
Independent kingdom since 1932.
Area: 2 240 000 square kms
Population: 10 421 000** (1983)
Capital: Riyadh

Syria
Republic since 1945; previously French mandated territory.
Area: 185 180 square kms
Population: 9 934 000* (1984)
Capital: Damascus

United Arab Emirates
Federation of seven independent emirates: Abu Dhabi, Ajman, Dubai, Fujaira, Ras al Khaimah, Sharja and Umm al Quwain.
Area: 77 700 square kms
Population: 1 622 464 (1985)
Capital: Abu Dhabi

North Yemen
Republic since 1962; previously monarchy since 1918.
Area: 200 000 square kms
Population: 7 161 851 (1985 census, excl. Yemenis abroad)
Capital: Sana'a

South Yemen
Popular democratic republic since 1967; previously British colony and protectorate.
Area: 336 869 square kms
Population: 2 225 000* (1984)
Capital: Aden

*Official estimate **UN estimate

Brief modern history

1916 Hussein, Sherif of Mecca, declares Arab independence. The Skyes-Picot agreement.

1917 Balfour Declaration on Palestine.

1918–19 Egyptian revolt against British occupation.

1920 British Mandate in Palestine.

1921 Faisal, son of Hussein of Mecca, declared King of Iraq.

1922 Egypt becomes sovereign state. Sultan Fuad king.

1923 State of Transjordan created.

1926 Ibn Saud seizes control of Mecca.

1932 Iraq declared independent state.

1936 Official end to British occupation of Egypt, though troops remain.

1936–38 Arabs revolt against British in Palestine.

1941 Muhammad Reza becomes Shah in Iran.

1946 Lebanese and Syrian independence established. Abdallah, son of Hussein of Mecca, becomes King of Transjordan.

1947 UN vote for partition in Palestine.

1948 End of British Mandate in Palestine. First Arab-Israeli war. Israel is established.

1952 Coup d'etat in Egypt. King exiled.

1956 Egypt seizes Suez Canal. Second Arab-Israeli war.

1958 Civil war in Lebanon. Coup d'etat in Iraq ends monarchy.

1964 First Palestinian National Council meeting, Jerusalem; PLO established.

1967 Third Arab-Israeli war.

1970 Fighting between the army and Palestinians in Jordan.

1973 Fourth Arab-Israeli war.

1974 Yasser Arafat, Chairman of PLO, addresses UN.

1975 Civil war in Lebanon.

1977 Sadat visits Israel.

1978 Camp David peace treaty signed.

1979 Shah of Iran exiled. Islamic republic established in Iran.

1980 War between Iran and Iraq.

1981 Sadat assassinated in Egypt.

1982 Israel invades Lebanon; withdraws under international pressure. Palestinian forces evacuate Beirut; civilian population of Sabra and Chatila Palestinian refugee camps massacred. International peacekeeping forces enter Beirut.

1986 America bombs Libya.

1987 Syrians re-enter Beirut.

Index

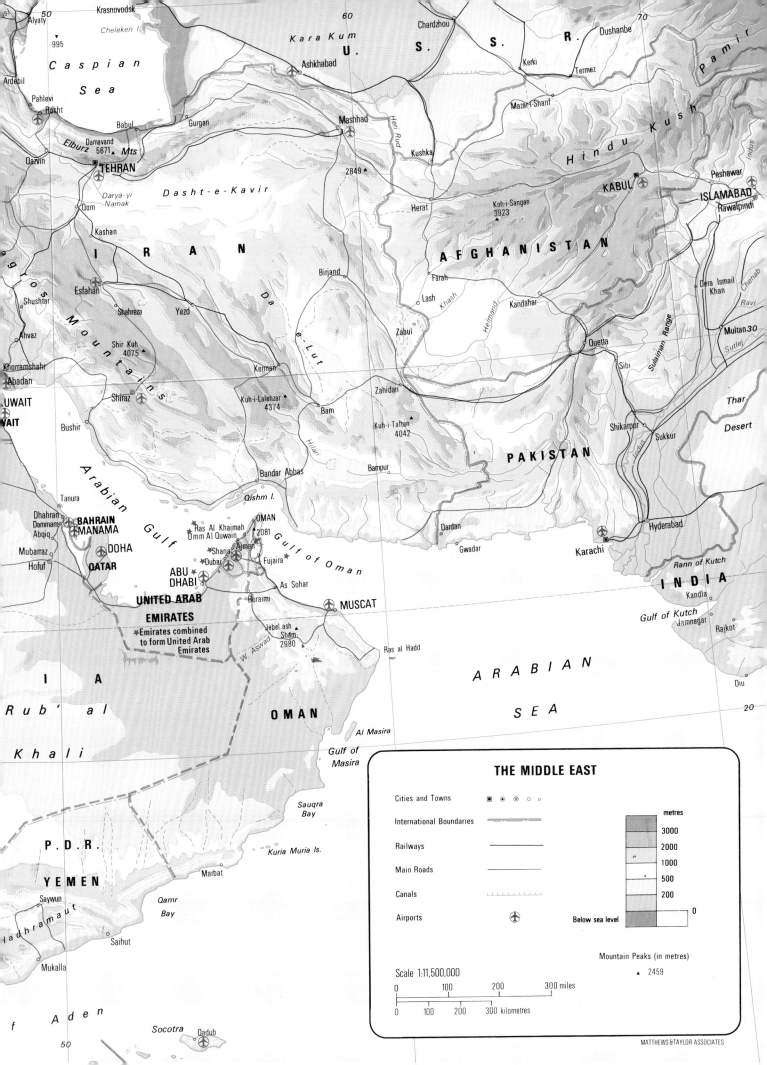

50
Krasnovodsk
Alyaty
Cheleken I.
-995
60
Kara Kum
Chardzhou
U. S.
S.
R.
70
Dushanbe
Ashkhabad
Kerki
Termez
Pamir

Ardebil
Caspian
Sea
Pahlevi
Rasht
Babul
Gurgan
Heri Rud
Mashhad
Kushka
Mazar-i-Sharif
Hindu Kush
Peshawar
ISLAMABAD
Rawalpindi

Elburz
Damavand
5671 ▲ Mts
Qazvin
TEHRAN
Qom
Darya-yi
Namak
Dasht-e-Kavir
2849 ▲
Herat
Koh-i-Sangan
3923
KABUL

Kashan
I
R
A
N
Birjand
Farah
AFGHANISTAN
Dera Ismail
Khan
Chenab
Ravi
30
Multan
Sutlej

Shushtar
Esfahan
Shahreza
Yezd
Lash
Khash
Ahvaz
Shir Kuh
4075 ▲
D
a
s
h
t
-
e
-
L
u
t
Zabul
Kandahar
Helmand
Quetta
Sibi
Sulaiman Range
Khorramshahr
Abadan
Kerman
Kuh-i-Lalehzar
4374 ▲
Bam
Zahidan
Kuh-i-Taftan
4042 ▲
Shikarpur
Sukkur
Thar
Desert
KUWAIT
AIT
Bushir
Shiraz
Z
a
g
r
o
s
M
o
u
n
t
a
i
n
s
Hilari
Bandar Abbas
Bampur
PAKISTAN
Indus
Hyderabad

Tanura
Qishm I.
Dardan
Gwadar
Karachi
Rann of Kutch
INDIA
Dhahran
Dammam
Abqiq
BAHRAIN
MANAMA
Arabian
Gulf
★ Ras Al Khaimah
Umm Al Quwain
OMAN
★ 2081
Gulf of Oman
Mubarraz
Hofuf
DOHA
QATAR
★ Sharja
Ajman
Dubai
Fujaira
As Sohar
Kandla
Gulf of Kutch
Jamnagar
ABU
DHABI
UNITED ARAB
EMIRATES
Buraimi
MUSCAT
Rajkot

I
A
IA
★ Emirates combined
to form United Arab
Emirates
Jebel ash
Sham ▲
2980
W. Aswad
Ras al Hadd
A R A B I A N
Diu

Rub' al
Khali
OMAN
S E A
20

Al Masira
Gulf of
Masira

Sauqra
Bay

THE MIDDLE EAST

Cities and Towns   ▣ ⊙ ◎ ○ ○

International Boundaries ━━━━━━

Railways   ━━━━━━

Main Roads   ━━━━━━

Canals   ⊢⊢⊢⊢⊢⊢

Airports   ✈

metres
3000
2000
1000
500
200
Below sea level
0

Mountain Peaks (in metres)
▲ 2459

Scale 1:11,500,000
0   100   200   300 miles
0 100 200 300 kilometres

P. D. R.
YEMEN
Saywun
Hadhramaut
Mukalla
Kuria Muria Is.
Marbat
Qamr
Bay
Saihut

f
Aden
50
Socotra
Qadub